Padua

Venice

N

Galileo's Journal
1609~1610

Jeanne K. Pettenati

Illustrated by Paolo Rui

Galileo lived in Italy 400 years ago. He was very curious and liked doing experiments to test his ideas. This book imagines what he might have written in his journal from July 1609 through March 1610. In those nine short months, Galileo made some of the most amazing discoveries in history.

✠ Charlesbridge

July 30, 1609, Venice

This morning I said good-bye to my students for the summer. As soon as they left, I hurried home to grab my bags. Then I hopped on a boat to Venice. Luna was so excited she barked all the way there.

Later I ate dinner at my friend Paolo's house. Paolo told me he had heard about an amazing new invention: a tube for seeing things far away. The tube has eyeglass lenses inside it, and it makes far-off things look like they are right in front of you. The Dutchman who invented this thing calls it a spyglass.

I wish I could try a spyglass for myself.

4

August 1, 1609, Venice

I struck several sour notes on my lute this morning. I couldn't stop thinking about that spyglass. I'm going to try to make one.

I need a long tube, to focus my eye on a faraway object without distractions. I also need glass lenses to go inside the tube.

How long should the tube be, I wonder? How many lenses do I need?

August 3, 1609, Padua

I arrived home yesterday and went right to work on my spyglass.
I began with just one curved lens in the tube. That didn't work.
A concave lens makes objects look smaller. A convex lens makes
objects look larger, but they are blurry and out of focus.
Then I tried using two lenses together. I put a concave lens close
to my eye and a convex lens at the far end of a tube. There it was!
Trees, houses, people, and animals all leaped toward me.

Single concave

Double concave

Double convex

Single convex

Concave lens

Outer tube slides to adjust distance between lenses

Convex lens

Inner tube

My spyglass makes things seem three times closer and nine times bigger. When I looked down into my garden, I saw two rabbits eating my lettuce! Where is that Luna when you need her?

August 19, 1609, Padua

Today I made my spyglass stronger by increasing the curve of the lenses. Distant objects now seem 60 times larger.

I am returning to Venice tomorrow. Luna can't come because I will be too busy. I am going to show my spyglass to the senators of the city!

August 21, 1609, Venice

This morning I took the senators to the top of St. Mark's tower, the highest point in the city. They looked through the spyglass at a tower in the town of Padua, 35 miles away. Then they looked across the water to an island and saw tiny people marching into a church. Finally, they spotted two ships far off at sea. Through the spyglass, the ships seemed close enough to touch.

"Extraordinary!" one senator cried. "Are they real?"

August 25, 1609, Venice

The senators are very pleased. With the spyglass, the navy will be able to spot ships long before they arrive in Venice. No enemy will be able to mount a surprise attack on the city.

The senators have doubled my teaching salary and appointed me professor for life. They even gave me a bonus sum, which I will use to buy more glass. Perhaps I will be able to make an even better spyglass.

My friends are taking me out to dinner to celebrate.

August 28, 1609, Padua

After a week of excitement, I am home again. Luna missed me.

September 15, 1609, Padua

My afternoons are filled with students, who come for
their lessons AND to see the spyglass. Mornings and evenings
I work on the spyglass—now it makes faraway objects seem
100 times larger.

With the spyglass, the navy can spot enemy
ships. Sailors at sea can keep an eye out for
pirates. But there must be other uses for
this amazing tool. What could they be?

I tried looking at things up
close, but that didn't work.
All I saw was a blur.

11

September 18, 1609, Padua

After dinner Luna and I went out in the garden. The first
stars of evening were beginning to shine. They looked so
beautiful and so tiny. Luna began barking at the moon.
Suddenly I had an idea. I grabbed my spyglass
and ran up to the rooftop.

I turned my spyglass to the moon, and my mouth dropped open.

People have always said that the moon is perfectly round, with a smooth surface like polished marble. Now I know the truth! The moon has mountains, valleys, and craters, just like Earth. I must be the first person ever to see them.

I watched the moon until it set. Now my arms are wobbly from holding the spyglass all night. I'm tired but too excited to sleep.

As a boy, I dreamed of walking on the moon. Tonight I traveled there!

13

October 15, 1609, Padua

    Through the spyglass, the stars look brighter. There are many more stars than people think. Hundreds, maybe even thousands more.

    With only my eyes, the Milky Way looks like a cloudy band of light stretching across the night sky. But the spyglass tells a different story. It shows that the Milky Way is made up of countless stars, so close to each other that their light blends together. I wonder why there are so many stars all grouped in harmony.

    I am discovering so much, yet so many mysteries remain.

October 20, 1609, Florence

Prince Cosimo has invited me to his palace to show him my spyglass. I used to tutor the prince when he was a boy. Now young Cosimo is the ruler of all Tuscany.

October 21, 1609, Florence

At the palace, we sat down to a grand feast. The tables were filled with caviar, roasted meats, salted fish, baked pears, and almond pastries. I had more than a little of everything.

As soon as darkness came, we went to the courtyard to look at the night sky. Prince Cosimo marveled at all we saw. Without my spyglass, even a prince cannot see the millions of stars twinkling across the Milky Way.

November 28, 1609, Padua

News travels quickly in this day and age. Letters are arriving from people all over the world. Some call me a hero. Others say, "Galileo is a liar! His spyglass is a fake!" A few even say that I put little pictures inside my spyglass to trick people. Ha!

These people don't believe that I see mountains on the moon. They have looked at the same moon year after year and never seen such a thing.

Why are they afraid to see what's really there?

December 8, 1609, Padua

So many people refuse to listen to me. But I won't give up.
I'll show them how incredible the night sky is.

Every day I think of some way to make the spyglass better.
I built a stand to hold it steady. Now I can turn it to look at
different parts of the sky. Bigger, better lenses also help—
distant objects now look 1,000 times larger.

Over the last few nights, I have watched sunlight sweep
across the moon, lighting up mountains and valleys. Observing
the shadows and light, I used geometry to figure out that some
of the moon's mountains are four miles high—higher than any
mountains on Earth!

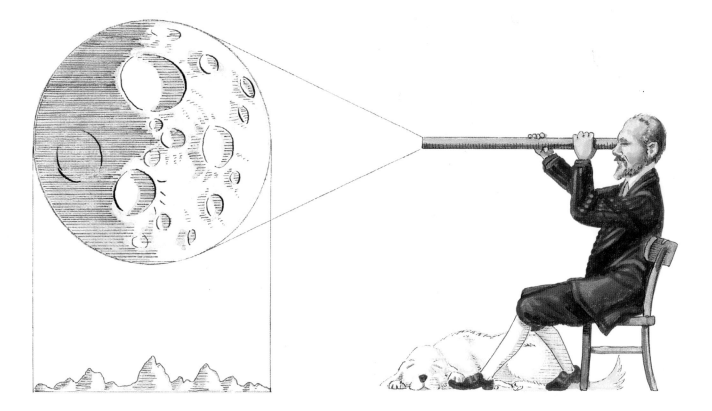

January 1, 1610, Padua

Happy New Year! Firecrackers are popping in the street. The smoke makes it hard to see the stars, so I'll just go outside and join the celebration.

Loud noises frighten Luna. She is hiding under my bed.

E

W

Looking South

January 7, 1610, Padua

The new year brings a new mystery.
Jupiter is so bright tonight that I noticed it right away.
Through the spyglass, I noticed something else. Three small,
very bright stars are lined up with Jupiter. Two stars are to the
east of the planet, and one star is to the west—all in a row.
What an odd formation!

Tonight I am looking again at Jupiter and those three bright stars—but now all three stars are west of Jupiter!

East  West

How can this be? Jupiter moves westward from night to night against a background of stars. The planet should have moved to the west of the three stars. Yet there it is, to the east. What is going on?

January 9, 1610, Padua

It is cloudy tonight. I cannot see Jupiter and that strange pattern of stars.

The changing formation from one night to the next puzzles me. Planets move in space, but stars do not. Are Jupiter and these stars connected in some way? How could they be?

My mind won't rest until I figure out this puzzle. But all Luna wants to do is go out and play.

21

January 10, 1610, Padua

Two of the bright stars are next to Jupiter tonight—but now both are to the east of the planet. Where is number three? Perhaps it is hidden from view behind the planet. Is that possible?

East   ✳   ✳   ◯   West

4:00 AM . . . Cannot sleep. Have been thinking—planets move and stars stay still. . . . But these stars do not stay still. . . . I wonder . . .

What if these stars and Jupiter are ALL moving? What if the stars move around Jupiter the way the moon moves around our Earth? Then what I see are not stars at all—they are moons!

I never thought another planet could have a moon. It doesn't seem possible that a planet could have three moons.

January 11, 1610, Padua   East   ✳ ✳ ⬤   West

Tonight I can see only two "moons"—both east of Jupiter.
I believe number three is behind Jupiter. If there are three
moons again tomorrow, I'll know for sure that these moons
go around and around Jupiter.

I have no patience—I can't wait for tomorrow night!
Thank goodness for Luna. While other people and their dogs
are sleeping peacefully, she is my constant companion. I take
a deep breath and warm my hands in her fur. It helps me think
more clearly.

January 12, 1610, Padua

1:00 AM—Two moons, one to the east of Jupiter and one to the west.

3:00 AM—Another moon comes into view east of Jupiter.

Now I am certain—they are MOONS circling their planet!

24

January 13, 1610, Padua

Oh magnificent night sky—you have revealed another secret!

There are FOUR moons! All week I could see only three. Jupiter's fourth moon must have been behind the planet and hidden from my view. But now I see four!

25

January 30, 1610, Padua

For weeks I have carefully observed Jupiter and its four bright moons. There can be no doubt about it. Jupiter has moons that orbit around it.

This changes everything!

Most people believe that the Earth is the center of the universe. They think that it stands still while the moon, sun, and planets move around it.

But the spyglass shows that the Earth is not the only center of motion in the universe. The Earth and Jupiter both have moons that travel around them.

Jupiter does not stand still—it moves as all the other planets do. If Jupiter can move in space with its moons, then so can Earth!

Here is evidence of what I have long suspected: all the planets, even Earth, move in space around the SUN.

January 31, 1610, Padua

The spyglass has helped me see what no one has ever seen before. I am writing a book to share my discoveries with the world. I will call the book *The Starry Messenger*. As a messenger from the stars, I will tell everyone about the wonders I have seen.

March 13, 1610, Padua

The Starry Messenger is now published. Orders for my
book are coming in every day. People near and far want to read
the news for themselves.

When I first made my spyglass, I thought it would be useful
for soldiers and sailors. I never imagined that it could bring
people on Earth closer to the stars.

I still travel the starry sky every night with Luna at my side.
With my spyglass, I'll continue to be a starry messenger.
This is just the beginning!

The Life of Galileo

Galileo Galilei was born on February 15, 1564, in Pisa, Italy. At the age of 17, Galileo enrolled in the University of Pisa and began studying medicine and mathematics. Later, he became a mathematics professor and a private tutor. One of his students was Prince Cosimo de Medici II of the powerful and influential Medici family.

Galileo is considered the father of modern science. He performed experiments to see if an idea was correct. Today scientists do this all the time. But in Galileo's time, many scholars simply believed things because people had accepted them as true for centuries.

Galileo wrote about his discoveries with the spyglass (later called the telescope) in his first book, *The Starry Messenger* (1610). Many people were impressed by the ideas in the book, but some were furious. Galileo's discovery that Jupiter had four moons challenged the popular belief that everything in the universe moved around Earth. People accused Galileo of disturbing the order of things.

After publishing *The Starry Messenger*, Galileo continued to use his spyglass to see what had never been seen before. He discovered sunspots on the face of the sun and observed the phases of Venus.

In 1632 Galileo wrote a book entitled *Dialogue Concerning the Two Chief World Systems*. In this book, he showed with logic and humor that the astronomer Nicolaus Copernicus (1473–1543) was right: the sun is the center of the solar system, and all the planets orbit around it.

In 1633 religious leaders in Rome accused Galileo of teaching a forbidden view of the universe. Galileo was allowed to return to his home in Florence, but he was not allowed to travel or teach anymore. He continued working on his experiments and receiving visitors until he died on January 8, 1642.

Today scientists, historians, and religious leaders agree that Galileo unlocked many of the secrets of our universe. The four largest moons of Jupiter are called the Galilean moons in his honor.

Author's Note

Most of the things I write about in this book really happened. In 1609 Galileo lived in Padua, where he was a professor of mathematics at the university. He grew fruits and vegetables in his garden, played the lute, and invented things in his workshop. When he wasn't working, Galileo often visited his good friend Paolo Sarpi in Venice. Paolo told Galileo about the spyglass.

Galileo really did climb up to the top of St. Mark's tower to show off his spyglass to the senators. They were so impressed that they doubled his teaching salary. Galileo continued to make dramatic improvements to his spyglass over a short period of time.

One autumn night in 1609, Galileo became the first person to use a telescope to explore the night sky. He kept notes and sketches of his observations. The dates for his discoveries about the moons of Jupiter come directly from his book *The Starry Messenger*.

Galileo liked to eat well and had a sweet tooth. He also seemed to like animals. He kept a little mule, which he treated very well. I don't know if Galileo had a pet dog, but the Italian sheepdog was a pet in Italian households during his lifetime.

The settings and science in the book are factual. I used my imagination to create Galileo's thoughts and dialogue, based on Galileo's own works and the research I conducted in writing this book.

Bibliography

Del Vecchio, Marisa, ed. *Bel Vedere: The Spectacles of the Luxottica Museum*. Vol. 1. Grafiche Antiga: Cornuda, Italy, 1999.

Ebbighausen, E. G. *Astronomy*. Columbus, OH: Charles E. Merrill Publishing Co., 1985.

Galilei, Galileo. *Discoveries and Opinions of Galileo*. Translated with an introduction and notes by Stillman Drake. Garden City, NY: Doubleday, 1957.

Galilei, Galileo. *Sidereus Nuncius*. 1610. http://www.liberliber.it/biblioteca/g/galilei/sidereus_nuncius/html/nunzio.htm. Available in English as *Sidereus Nuncius, or The Sidereal Messenger*. Translated by Albert Van Helden. Chicago: University of Chicago Press, 1989.

Galilei, Maria Celeste. *Letters to Father: Suor Maria Celeste to Galileo, 1623–1633*. Translated and annotated by Dava Sobel. New York: Walker & Company, 2001.

Panek, Richard. *Seeing and Believing: How the Telescope Opened Our Eyes and Minds to the Heavens*. New York: Viking, 1998.

Reston, James, Jr. *Galileo: A Life*. New York: HarperCollins, 1994.

Ronan, Colin A. *Galileo*. New York: G. P. Putnam's Sons, 1974.

Sobel, Dava. *Galileo's Daughter: A Historical Memoir of Science, Faith, and Love*. New York: Walker & Company, 1999.

For my little "stars," Haley and Matthew, and my husband, Alan.
For my parents also, and my brother, Al. Grazie.—J. K. P.

To my wife, Vicky, and our child, Leo, goldmines of inspiration and glee,
and to my father, who shared my enthusiasm when I started the book,
but didn't have a chance to see its end. Ciao.—P. R.

Special thanks to R. Bruce Ward and Sam Palmer of the
Harvard-Smithsonian Center for Astrophysics.

Published by Charlesbridge
85 Main Street, Watertown, MA 02472
(617) 926-0329
www.charlesbridge.com

Library of Congress Cataloging-in-Publication Data
Pettenati, Jeanne.
Galileo's journal, 1609-1610 / Jeanne K. Pettenati ; illustrated by Paolo Rui.
p. cm.
Includes bibliographical references.
Summary: This fictional journal is from the year in which Galileo constructed his own telescope and began to record his astronomical discoveries. Includes additional nonfiction biographical information.
ISBN-13: 978-1-57091-879-7; ISBN-10: 1-57091-879-1 (reinforced for library use)
ISBN-13: 978-1-57091-880-3; ISBN-10: 1-57091-880-5 (softcover)
1. Galileo, 1564-1642—Juvenile fiction. [1. Galileo, 1564-1642—Fiction. 2. Inventors—Fiction. 3. Telescopes—Fiction.] I. Rui, Paolo, ill. II. Title.
PZ7.P44807Gal 2006
[Fic]—dc22   2005003911

Printed in China
(hc)   10 9 8 7 6 5 4 3 2 1
(sc)   10 9 8 7 6 5 4 3 2 1

Pisa

Florence